PLACES IN THE COMMUNITY

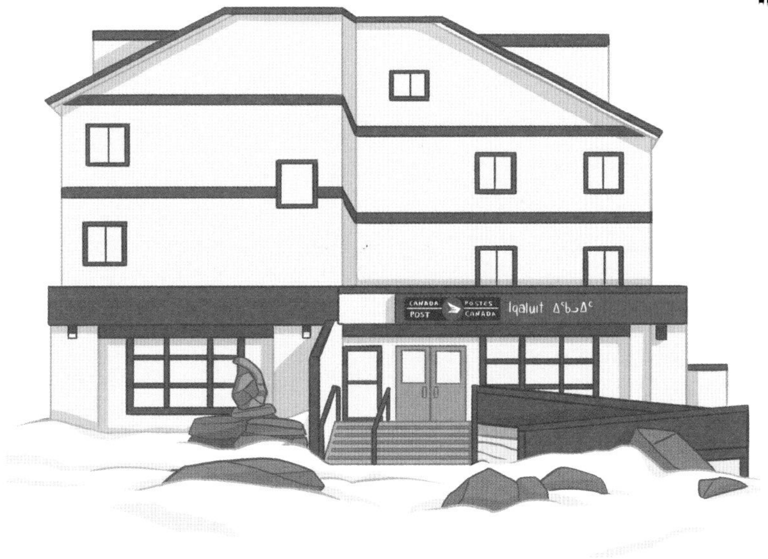

ILLUSTRATED BY

Amanda Sandland

school

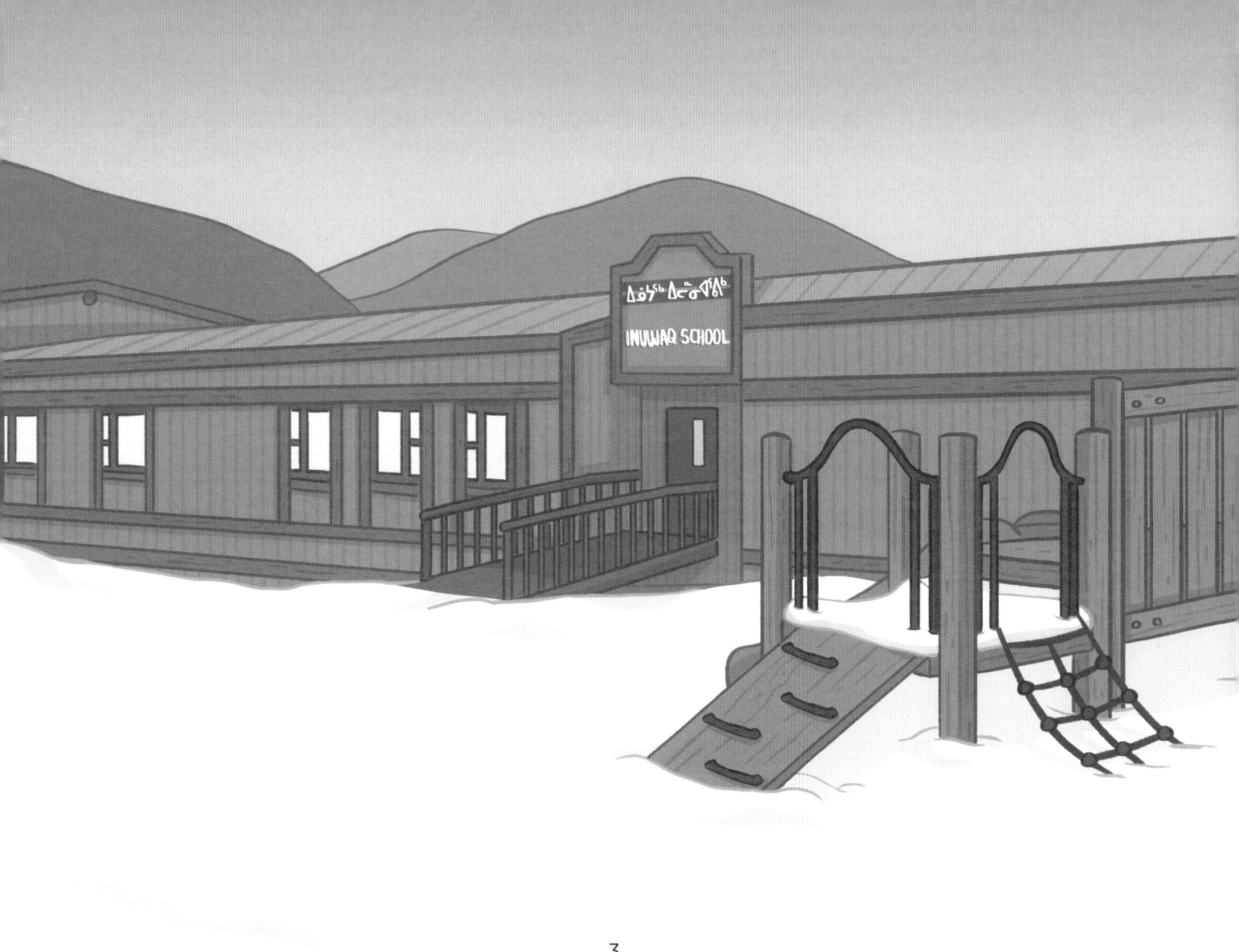
ᐃᓅᔮᖅ ᐃᓕᓐᓂᐊᕐᕕᒃ
INUUJAQ SCHOOL

health centre

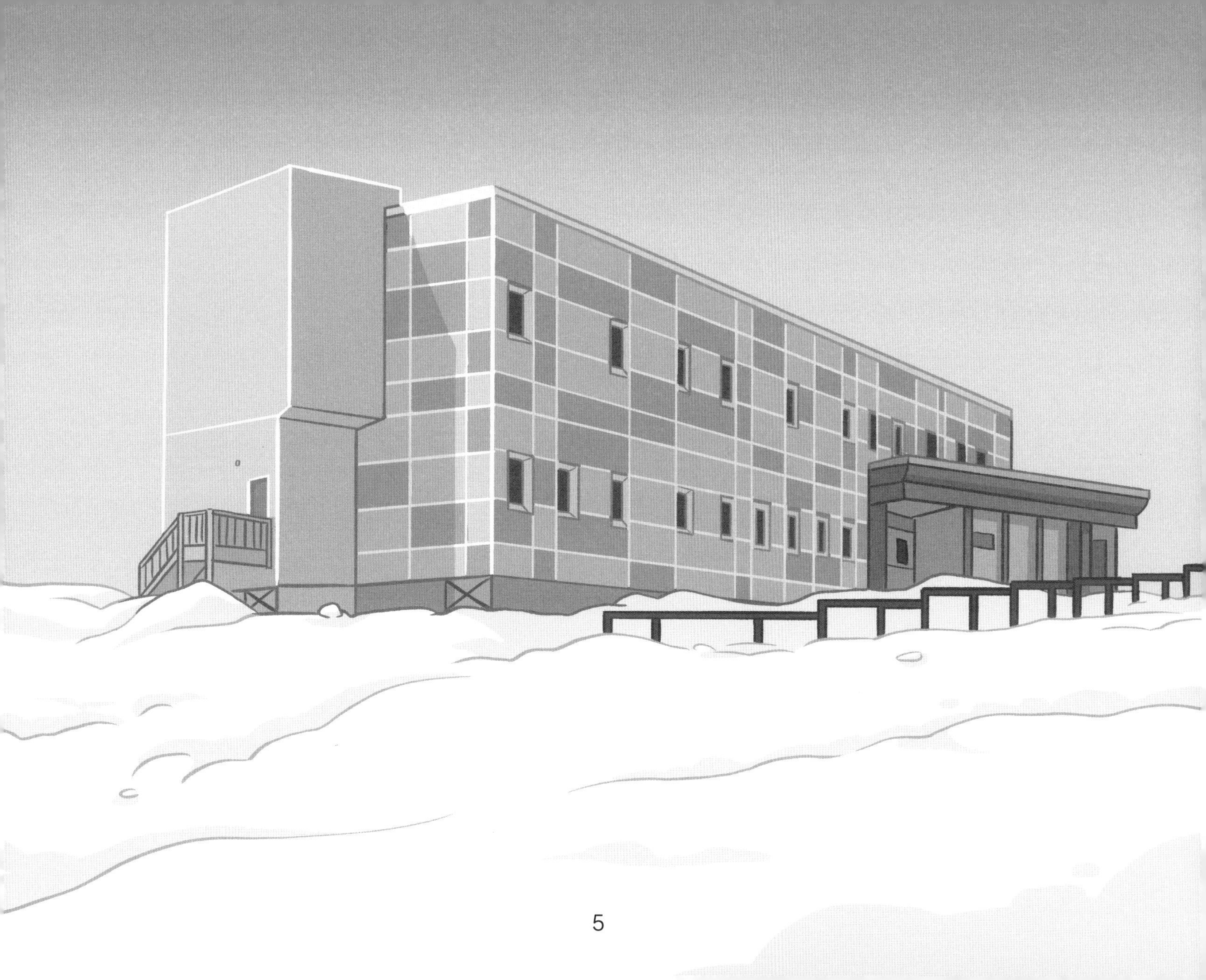

community centre

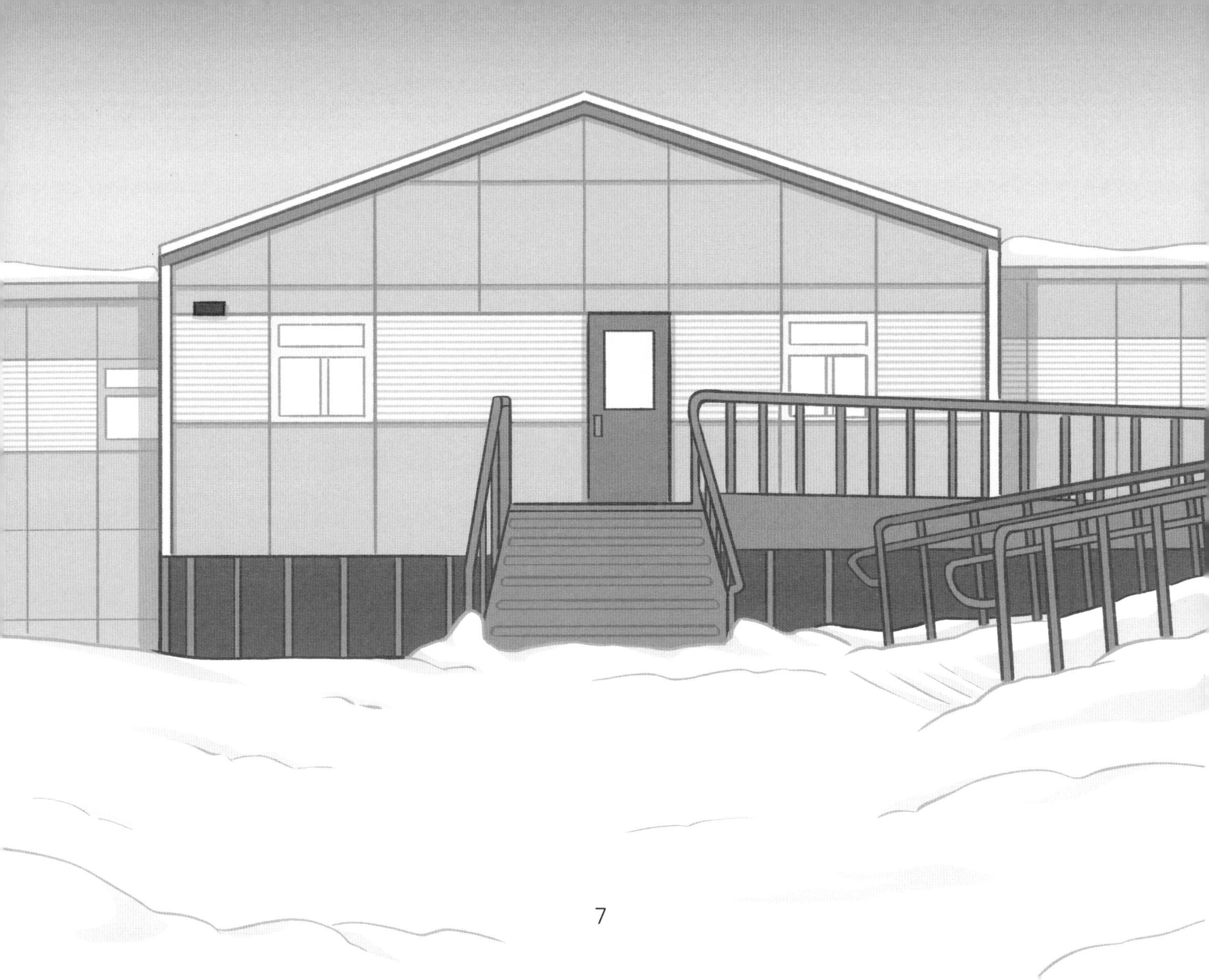

post office

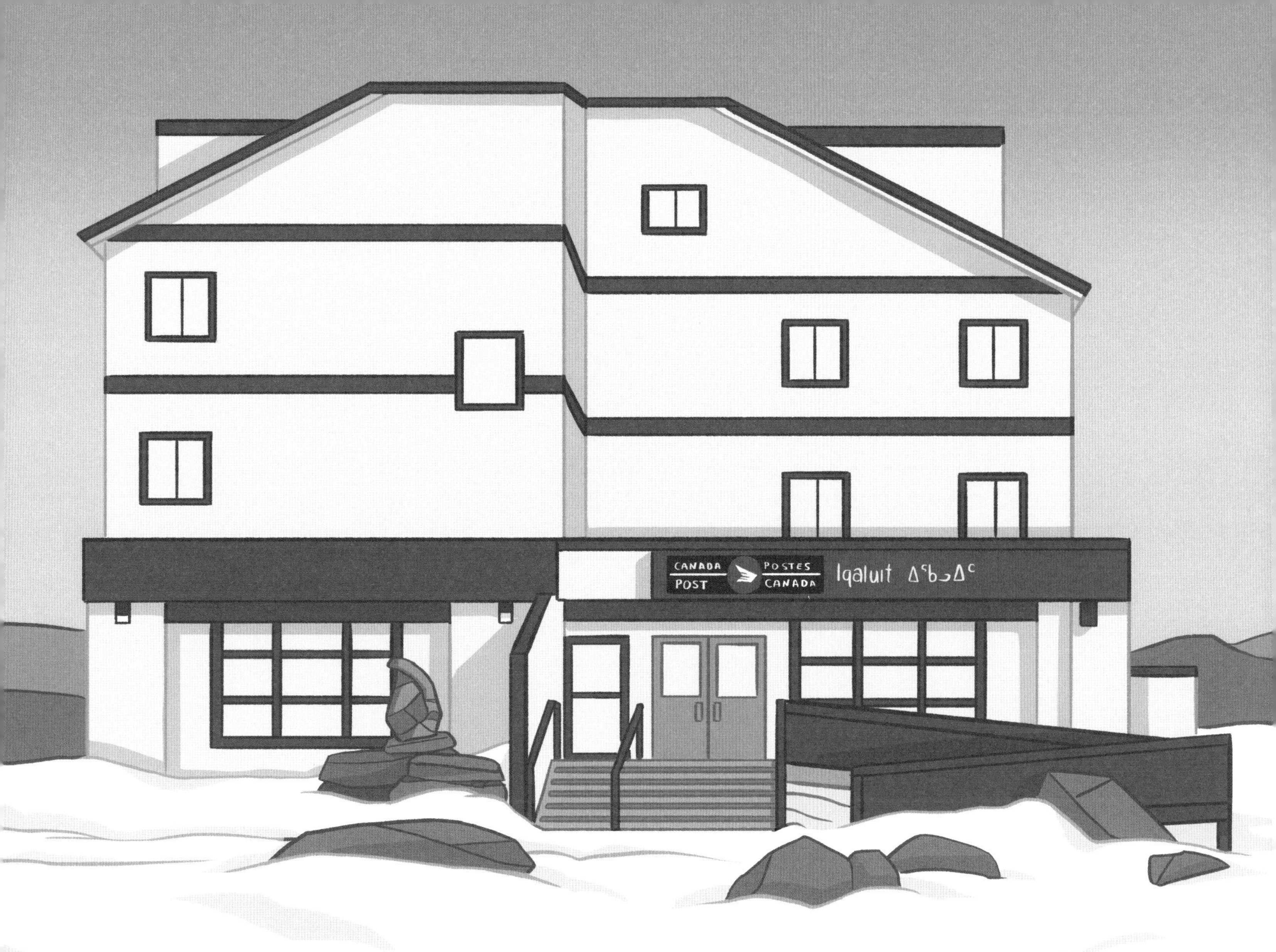
CANADA POST
POSTES CANADA
Iqaluit ᐃᖃᓗᐃᑦ

church

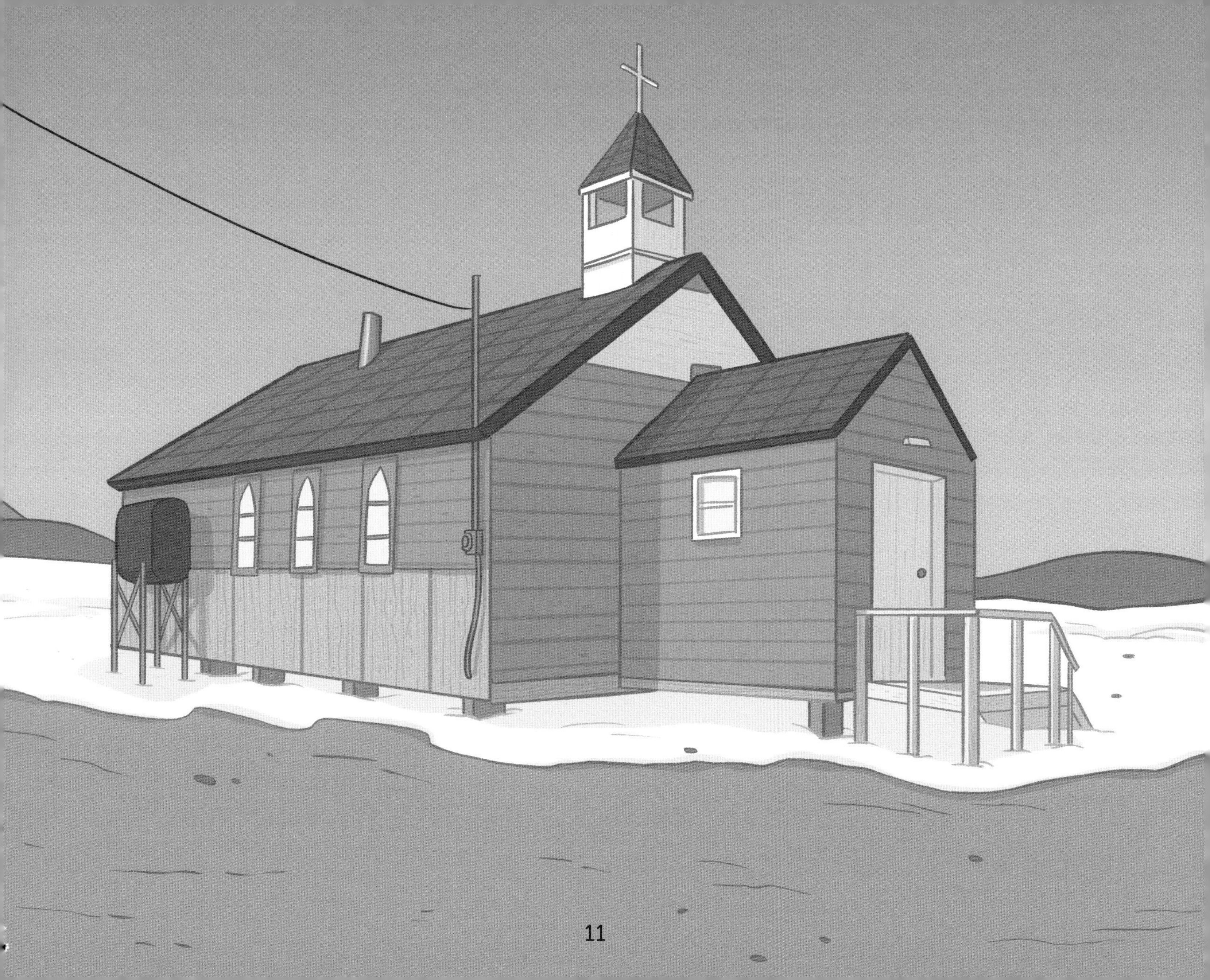

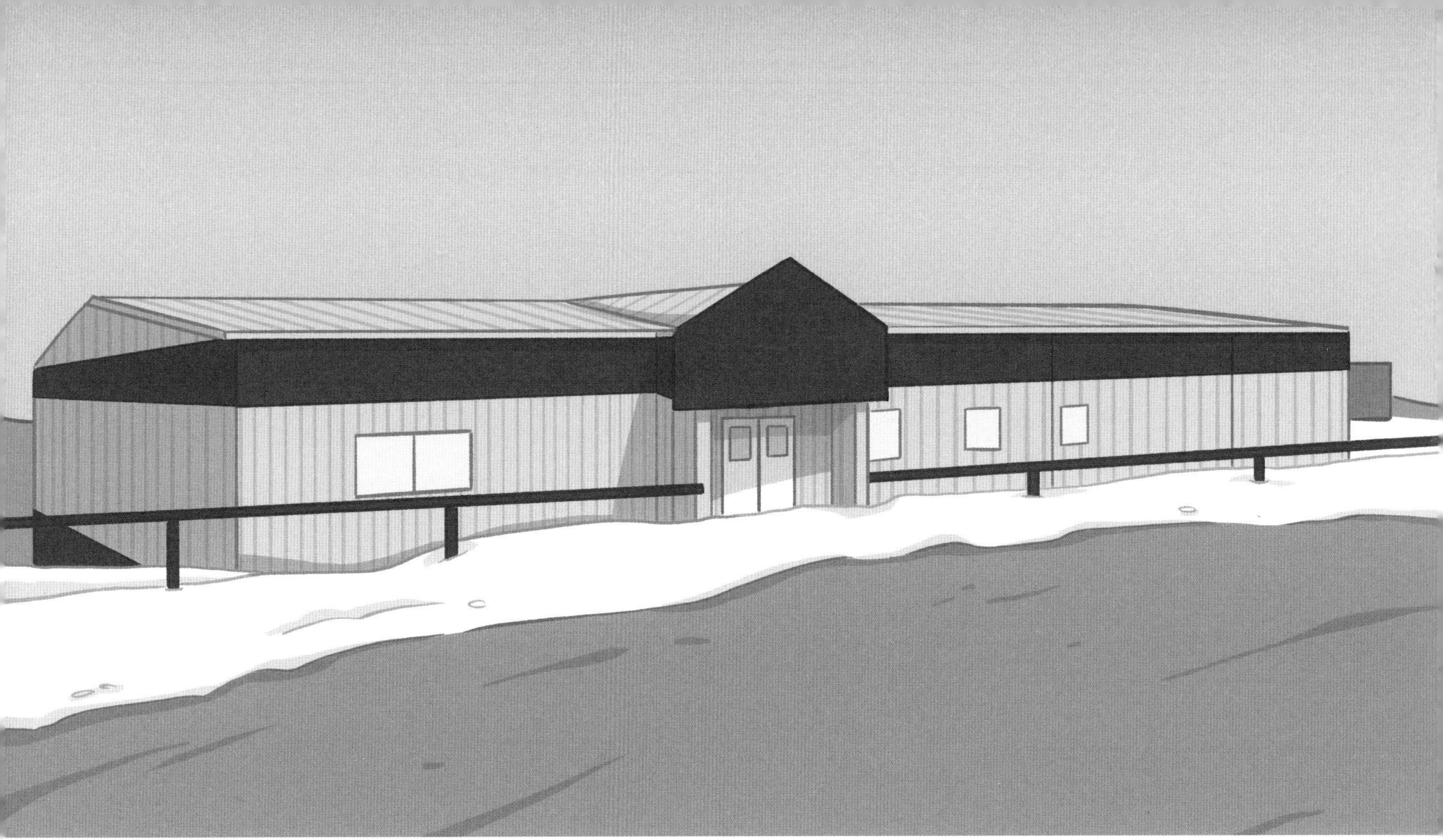

store